ANIMALS
That Make a Difference!

Squirrels
Ardillas

Ashley Lee

Explore other books at:
WWW.ENGAGEBOOKS.COM

VANCOUVER, B.C.

e→ WWW.ENGAGEBOOKS.COM

Squirrels: Level 1 Bilingual (English/Spanish) (Ingles/Español)
Animals That Make a Difference!
Lee, Ashley 1995 –
Text © 2021 Engage Books
Edited by: A.R. Roumanis and Lauren Dick
Translated by: Juan Ortega Aliaga
Proofread by: Andrés Cordero

Text set in Arial Regular.
Chapter headings set in Arial Black.

FIRST EDITION / FIRST PRINTING

LIBRARY AND ARCHIVES CANADA CATALOGUING IN PUBLICATION

Title: Animals That Make a Difference: Squirrels Level 1 Bilingual (English / Spanish) (Ingles / Español)
Names: Lee, Ashley, author.

ISBN 978-1-77476-402-2 (hardcover)
ISBN 978-1-77476-401-5 (softcover)

Subjects:
LCSH: Squirrels—Juvenile literature
LCSH: Human-animal relationships—Juvenile literature

Classification: LCC QL737.R68 L44 2020 | DDC J599.36—DC23

Contents Contenidos

What Are Squirrels?
Qué son las ardillas?

Squirrels are rodents.
Las ardillas son roedores.

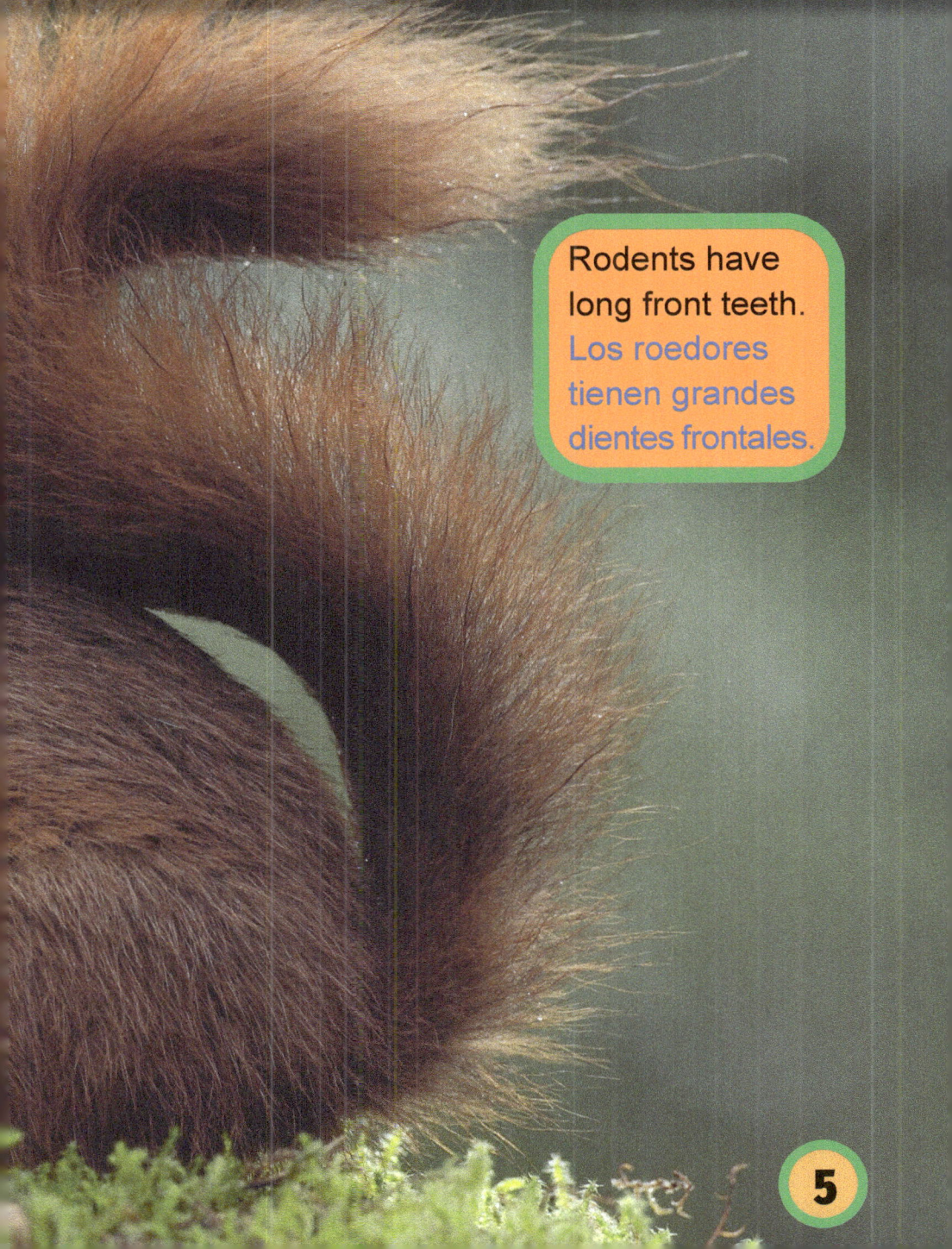

Rodents have long front teeth.
Los roedores tienen grandes dientes frontales.

What Do Squirrels Look Like?
Cómo se ven las ardillas?

The largest squirrels are 3 feet (1 meter) long from their nose to the end of their tail. The smallest squirrels are only 5 inches (13 centimeters) long.

Las ardillas más grandes son de 3 pies (1 metro) de largo desde su nariz hasta el final de su cola. Las ardillas más pequeñas son de apenas 5 pulgadas (13 centímetros) de largo.

A squirrel's tail is long and bushy.
La cola de una ardilla es larga y frondosa.

Squirrels have sharp front teeth that never stop growing.

Las ardillas tienen dientes frontales afilados que nunca dejan de crecer.

Squirrels have four fingers on each front paw. They also have short thumbs for gripping.

Las ardillas tienen 4 dedos en cada pata. También tienen dedos pulgares cortos para sujetarse.

Where Do Squirrels Live?
Dónde viven las ardillas?

Squirrels live all over the world. The only place they are not found is in Australia. Some squirrels live in trees and some live underground.

Las ardillas viven en todo el mundo. El único lugar en donde no se las encuentra es en Australia. Algunas ardillas viven en árboles y otras bajo tierra.

Three-striped palm squirrels are found in India and Sri Lanka. Japanese dwarf flying squirrels can only be found in Japan.

Las ardillas de palma de tres rayas viven en la India y en Sri Lanka. Las ardillas voladoras enanas solo se pueden encontrar en Japón.

Arctic Ocean
Océano Ártico

Japan
Japón

Europe
Europa

India
India

Asia
Asia

Africa
África

Pacific Ocean
Océano Pacífico

Atlantic Ocean
Océano Atlántico

Indian Ocean
Océano Índico

Sri Lanka
Sri Lanka

Southern Ocean
Océano Antártico

2,000 miles
2,000 millas
0

4,000 kilometers
4,000 kilómetros
0

N

Legend Leyenda
Land Tierra
Ocean Océano

9

What Do Squirrels Eat?
Qué comen las ardillas?

Squirrels mostly eat nuts, seeds, and plants. They also eat small insects, fruit, and tree sap.

Las ardillas comen mayormente nueces, semillas, y plantas. Ellas también comen pequeños insectos, fruta, y savia de árbol.

Some squirrels hide their food. They bury it in the soil for later.

Algunas ardillas esconden su comida. La entierran bajo el suelo para comerla más tarde.

How Do Squirrels Talk to Each Other?

Cómo se comunican las ardillas entre ellas?

Squirrels make sounds to call other squirrels or warn them of danger. Some squirrels will scream when they are scared.

Las ardillas hacen sonidos para llamar a otras ardillas o advertirles del peligro. Algunas ardillas gritarán si están asustadas.

Squirrels wave their tails back and forth when they are attacked. This makes them look bigger and can scareother animals.

Las ardillas agitan sus colas de un lado para el otro cuando son atacadas. Esto las hace ver más grandes y pueden espantar a otros animales.

Squirrel Life Cycle
El ciclo de vida de la ardilla

Baby squirrels are born hairless and blind. Their eyes stay closed for about one month.
Las ardillas bebés nacen sin pelo y ciegas. Sus ojos permanecen cerrados por casi un mes.

Young squirrels cannot leave their mother's nest for about 40 days.
Las ardillas jóvenes no pueden dejar el nido de sus madres por casi 40 días.

Young squirrels make their own nests when they are about two months old.

Las ardillas jóvenes hacen su propio nido cuando tienen casi dos meses de edad.

Some types of squirrels live longer than others. Eastern gray squirrels can live for up to 12 years. Tiny antelope ground squirrels only live for about one year.

Algunos tipos de ardillas viven más tiempo que otros. Las ardillas grises orientales pueden vivir hasta 12 años. Las diminutas ardillas antílope de tierra solo viven alrededor de un año.

Curious Facts About Squirrels

Some squirrels sort their food into groups before burying it. They may sort their nuts by type or size.
Algunas ardillas clasifican su comida en grupos antes de enterrarla. Pueden clasificar sus nueces por tipo o tamaño.

Squirrels sometimes pretend to bury their nuts. This is meant to trick any thieves who may be watching.
Las ardillas algunas veces simulan enterrar sus nueces. Esto significa que engañan a cualquier ladrón que las esté observando.

Squirrels can find their buried food under one foot of snow.
Las ardillas pueden encontrar su comida enterrada a un pie bajo nieve.

Datos curiosos acerca de las ardillas

Some squirrels have pouches in their cheeks for storing food.
Algunas ardillas tienen bolsas en sus cachetes para almacenar la comida.

Squirrels are one of the few animals that can run down a tree head first.
Las ardillas son uno de los pocos animales que pueden bajar de cabeza un árbol.

Squirrels were a common pet in North America about 200 years ago.
Las ardillas fueron una mascota común en Norteamérica hace 200 años.

17

Kinds of Squirrels
Tipos de ardillas

There are more than 250 different kinds of squirrels. These are split into three groups. The squirrels in each group are similar.

Hay más de 250 tipos distintos de ardillas. Estos están divididos en tres grupos. Las ardillas en cada grupo son similares.

Tree squirrels are the most common type of squirrel. They live in trees and are great climbers.

Las ardillas de árbol son el tipo más común de ardillas. Ellas viven en árboles y son hábiles trepadoras.

Flying squirrels have a thin layer of skin between their front and back legs. This acts like a pair of wings when they jump between trees.

Las ardillas voladoras tienen una fina capa de piel entre sus patas delanteras y traseras. Esta actúa como un par de alas cuando saltan de árbol en árbol.

Ground squirrels live underground. They are often found in large groups.

Las ardillas terrestres viven bajo tierra. Ellas son frecuentemente vistas en grupos numerosos.

How Squirrels Help Other Animals

Cómo las ardillas ayudan a otros animales

Squirrels are food for other animals.

Las ardillas son alimento para otros animales.

There would be less wolves, snakes, and large birds without squirrels for them to eat.

Habría menos lobos, serpientes, y una cantidad menor de aves si no hubieran ardillas para comer.

How Squirrels Help Earth
Cómo las ardillas ayudan al planeta

Squirrels bury nuts and seeds in many different spots. Sometimes squirrels cannot remember where they hid their food.

Las ardillas entierran sus nueces y semillas en distintos lugares. Algunas veces las ardillas no pueden recordar dónde escondieron su comida.

Some buried nuts and seeds grow into new plants. Many plants would not grow without help from forgetful squirrels. Algunas nueces y semillas enterradas crecen y se convierten en nuevas plantas. Muchas plantas no crecerían sin la ayuda de las ardillas olvidadizas.

How Squirrels Help Humans
Cómo las ardillas ayudan a los seres humanos

Some squirrels hibernate during the winter. This means they sleep until the weather gets warmer.

Algunas ardillas hibernan durante el invierno. Esto significa que duermen hasta que el clima sea cálido.

Scientists are studying how squirrels hibernate. This may help them make new medicine for people with heart problems.

Los científicos están estudiando cómo las ardillas hibernan. Esto les ayudaría a producir una nueva medicina para personas con problemas cardíacos.

Squirrels in Danger
Ardillas en peligro

Red squirrels are endangered. This means there are very few of them left.

Las ardillas rojas están en peligro de extinción. Esto significa que solo quedan unas cuantas de ellas.

Red squirrels live in England, Wales, Ireland, and Scotland. Gray squirrels were brought to these countries from North America. They brought a germ with them that harms red squirrels.

Las ardillas rojas viven en Inglaterra, Gales, Irlanda, y Escocia. Las ardillas grises fueron traídas a esos países desde Norteamérica. Ellas trajeron un germen que daña a las ardillas rojas.

27

How To Help Squirrels
Cómo ayudar a las ardillas

Garbage can end up in places animals live. Squirrels can get hurt if they get trapped in a piece of garbage. They can also get sick if they try to eat it.

La basura puede terminar en lugares donde viven animales. Las ardillas pueden herirse si quedan atrapadas en desperdicios de basura. También se pueden enfermar si intentan comer estos desperdicios.

Many people are cleaning forests. They pick up garbage and take it to a landfill. This helps keep squirrels safe.

Muchas personas están limpiando los bosques. Ellos recogen los desperdicios y los llevan al vertedero. Esto ayuda a mantener a las ardillas a salvo.

Quiz
Cuestionario

Test your knowledge of squirrels by answering the following questions. The questions are based on what you have read in this book. The answers are listed on the bottom of the next page.

Pon a prueba tu conocimiento acerca de las ardillas respondiendo las siguientes preguntas. Estas preguntas están basadas en lo que leíste en este libro. Las respuestas están listadas al final de la siguiente página.

1 What is the only place squirrels are not found?
Cuál es el único lugar donde no se encuentran ardillas?

2 What do some squirrels do when they are scared?
Qué hacen algunas ardillas cuando están asustadas?

3 How long do a baby squirrel's eyes stay closed?
Por cuánto tiempo los ojos de las ardillas bebés permanecen cerrados?

4 How do squirrels sometimes trick thieves?
Cómo las ardillas engañan algunas veces a los ladrones?

5 How many different kinds of squirrels are there?
Cuántos tipos distintos de ardillas existen?

6 What does it mean when squirrels hibernate during winter
Qué significa cuando las ardillas hibernan durante el invierno?

Explore other books in the Animals That Make a Difference series.

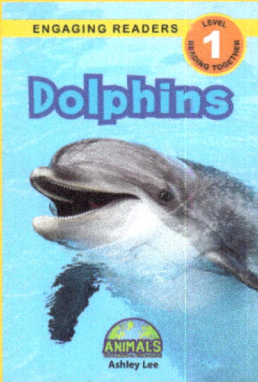

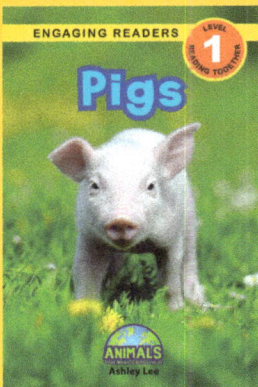

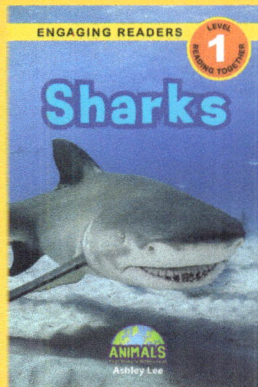

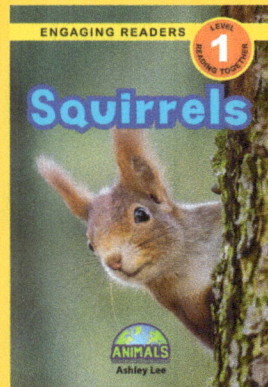

ENGAGING READERS — LEVEL 1 READING TOGETHER
Bees
ANIMALS
Jared Siemens

ENGAGING READERS — LEVEL 1 READING TOGETHER
Bats
ANIMALS
Ashley Lee

ENGAGING READERS — LEVEL 1 READING TOGETHER
Birds
ANIMALS
Ashley Lee

ENGAGING READERS — LEVEL 1 READING TOGETHER
Dolphins
ANIMALS
Ashley Lee

ENGAGING READERS — LEVEL 1 READING TOGETHER
Horses
ANIMALS
Ashley Lee

ENGAGING READERS — LEVEL 1 READING TOGETHER
Lady Bugs
ANIMALS
Ashley Lee

ENGAGING READERS — LEVEL 1 READING TOGETHER
Pigs
ANIMALS
Ashley Lee

ENGAGING READERS — LEVEL 1 READING TOGETHER
Sharks
ANIMALS
Ashley Lee

ENGAGING READERS — LEVEL 1 READING TOGETHER
Squirrels
ANIMALS
Ashley Lee

Visit www.engagebooks.com to explore more Engaging Readers.

Respuestas:
1. Australia 2. Gritan 3. Cerca de un mes 4. Ellas simulan enterrar sus nueces 5. Más de 250 6. Ellas duermen hasta que el clima sea cálido

Answers:
1. Australia 2. Scream 3. About one month 4. They pretend to bury their nuts 5. More than 250 6. They sleep until the weather gets warmer

www.ingramcontent.com/pod-product-compliance
Lightning Source LLC
Chambersburg PA
CBHW051240020426
42331CB00016B/3461